headfirst

Two passions intertwine.
A tangle of fantasies.
I make no attempt to unravel them.
They burn together like small coals,
sparking my imagination.

Hats & Poems by
Sylvia Fletcher

Withdrawn

When I was ten
I went to church in a hat
It was as simple as that

Collective work © New Cavendish Books. Text © Sylvia Fletcher. Hat designs © Sylvia Fletcher.
Sylvia Fletcher is hereby identified as the author of this work in accordance with Section 77
of the Copyright, Designs and Patents Act, 1988.

First published by New Cavendish Books, October 2009.
New Cavendish Books, 3 Denbigh Road, London W11 2SJ
T: +44 (0) 207 229 6765   E: sales@newcavendishbooks.co.uk   W: www.newcavendishbooks.co.uk

ISBN: 978 1 904562115

Printed and bound in Thailand

I made my grandmother a hat when I was twelve and she loved me enough to wear it.

As my creativity blossomed I rendered the contents of her china cabinet unusable, every slender stemmed glass, plate and fruit bowl I embellished with fruit flowers and family portraits, sealed inadequately with a coating of her clear nail polish.

I made Christmas gifts which were opened apprehensively by aunts and uncles and then displayed in a prime position for the minimal amount of time.

Felt comb cases that I made for uncles, I learned years later had always remained a mystery to them. They did not come with comb and so their purpose was open to conjecture.

My dream was to eventually attend art college, but it was necessary for me to contribute to the family income, so at sixteen I left school and became apprentice to a milliner in London.

The company was owned by Madame Sybil Pendlebury who was the oldest person I knew. She smelled of face powder and *Midnight in Paris*. Her long carmine lacquered nails were mostly occupied with over-feathering a variety of hats with ostrich plumes. They were identical once feathered and sat in rows like a flock of migrating birds. I developed an aversion to that particular feather.

Recently a client who had insisted on an ostrich trimmed hat was advised to store it in a cool place. We were pleased to learn from her later that she had given it to the butler to store in the pantry with the pheasant.

A hat is . . .
a cloak of mystery
a fanfare . . .

... an invitation.
Is the click of a high heel
and the waft of a powder puff...

PHOTO: DANILO GIULIANI

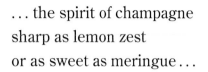

... the spirit of champagne
sharp as lemon zest
or as sweet as meringue ...

... a web of contradictions at my fingertips.
For a woman I provide the final brush stroke,
fulfill a longing, create a fantasy.
Then ... I pass him the bill.

PHOTO: JULIAN MARSHALL

CREAM

The shirt was cream.
    It made me different.
On my first day at big school,
    amongst the rows of identical
    grey and white uniforms
I was different.

It was beautifully made
    by my Mother
    but it was cream.
The shirt heralded my arrival
    like a fanfare from
    the Black Dyke Mills Band.

That shirt drew back heavy curtains,
    placed me centre stage
    and turned the spotlight full on.
That's when it all began.
    I had decisions to make.

PHOTOS: DANILO GIULIANI

BLUE TULIPS

Dare to be blue
Defiantly so
Shout a difference
Lack yellow or pink
Lift joyous heads
Bright blue
And laugh at the joke

MY COUSIN SANDRA

My second cousin was thin
   and went to ballet class.
Sandra was measured and tweaked,
   tulled and sequined.
Sandra's mother arched over her.
Our holiday treat?
Sandra in the chorus
   at Clacton Town Hall.
I longed to view the world
   perched on pink satin toes.
Has she teetered I wonder?

NEW GIRL

The lift opened exposing me to a full-length mirror. I winced. Beached like a jellyfish by inadequate ripples of education onto the rocky shores of employment and the world of fashion, I stepped into the millinery establishment of Madame Sybil Pendlebury.

I could not have appeared less suitably equipped for the position had I worn a pith helmet and safari suit. My first-day-at-work outfit was clean and neatly pressed, but was unmistakably my school uniform minus beret and tie.

My father had explained, at my request for a clothing loan, that money should be earned before it was spent and not the other way round. So that was that.

My comforting screen of long chestnut coloured hair had been submitted to the traditional 'starting work Dulcette Home Perm' and was now suitably transformed, to my despair, short and frizzed aggressively tight to last longer.

I was introduced to the designer Miss Brashby and her identical sister. From then on they proceeded from behind their fortress of sisterhood, to fire darts, throw spears and trickle boiling oil onto my 'Dulcette-permed' head for two years until I completed my apprenticeship and was offered a position as designer. At this point, as in all good fairy tales, the wicked genies departed in a wisp of smoke up their own identical spouts.

Sylvia (top left) with her apprentice milliners in the workroom in the early sixties.

PHOTO: SYLVIE TATA

FASHION SHOW AT THE RITZ

My mother wore the Ritz like an old pair of slippers. She was as much at ease there as any of the 'ladies that lunch' who had been invited to the show. At eighty-four years of age she had honed the skills of survival, learned to make a mince stew last for two days by adding dumpling and remake an aunt's donated dress into a school skirt or blouse. Her talents were endless and necessary.

I watched from the wings as models wearing my latest collection moved between the tables. Mother whilst savouring the selection of wafer thin sandwiches and iced fancies, was appraising each hat.

She wore her Sylvia Fletcher hat at just the right angle on her freshly permed hair and was wearing her new M&S jacket.

The final applause was for the collection, but for me my mother was the star of the show.

MISS NELLIE BROWN

Nellie makes our tea with the help of God,
    in porcelain cups bleached virginal white.

Our teaspoons bear the scratches of a good 'Vim-ing'
    as she sings of God's love tunelessly, as Nellie can't hear.

Thin and bent as one of her ineffectual hair pins,
    she counts the custard creams.
Two per person and one for luck (or for God I suspect)
    and arranges them in straight rows.

Nellie brightens her trolley with artificial flowers,
    a tea towel from Camber Sands and is our salvation.

SALESMAN SUPERIORE

Nigel is huge and soft, an ex-fighter
   who now rides the punches of the retail trade.
When Nigel displays his 'Superiore Fedoras' he is an artist.
He prises open the box slowly, savouring.
A gold seal is peeled away releasing sheets
   of black tissue to expose 'Superiore'.
He wipes the corner of his mouth
   with the third finger of his right hand,
     the sight of such a morsel moistening his taste buds.
Nigel cradles in his huge palms the object of his desire.
   the felt hat, fine as chamois.
He passes a breath across its surface to lift its peach-like bloom
   and places it into my hands to feel its weightlessness.

I am seduced.

Envelop me in chocolate.
Wrap me in cashmere.
Glistening bitter velvet
next to my skin.

PHOTO: DANILO GIULIANI

Melt in a tall glass,
Stir in double cream.
Stroke my taste buds.
My lip sinks in.

BUSINESS STRIP

I had been swept to France in the inspirational whirlwind that was Narangalos, my new Managing Director. I was allowed just enough time to grab a pair of heels and one of my little felt hats I thought Paris would love.

I was to introduce him to the joys of a feather artist's studios, the creators of silk flowers, millinery block makers whose workshops displayed polished wooden shapes that gleamed like conkers – and my beloved cloth houses.

Narangalos was armed with a list of contacts for the men's hat department and a box of the season's new tweed caps. He had a second list of restaurants and bars, which I agreed we should slot in between appointments. We returned to the hotel having completed both lists, having particularly enjoyed the second one.

I arrived at his room at 8am the following morning as agreed. I was surprised to see that he wasn't wearing a suit. In fact he wasn't wearing anything except rather a lot of hair and a white towel wrapped at the waist. He was modelling a deerstalker sample, earflaps and arms swinging wildly as he argued the fors and againsts of rain proofing it. His enthusiasm made him oblivious to his appearance and the fact that the towel was edging its way downwards. A demented Sherlock Holmes. I hurriedly agreed to rain proofing, definitely rain proofing and hastily left the room allowing him to rescue the towel, which by this time would be around his feet.

I waited for him in the lobby; it was the end of a business trip but the start of a love affair … with Paris.

LOVE

I stood beneath the Eiffel Tower.
Floodlights etched the metallic lacework.
A gilded spiders web.
I was caught in its spell,
like a moth.

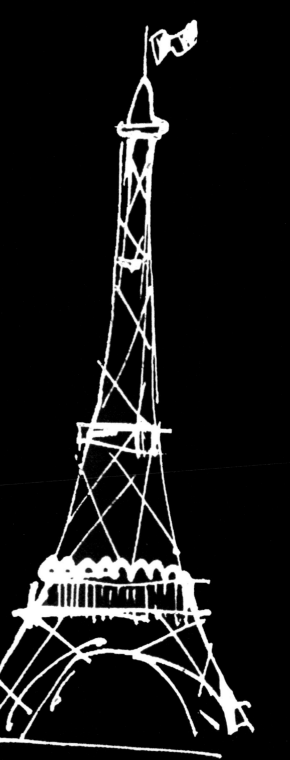

CLOTH

My greatest pleasure was buying fabrics in Paris, sitting on cellar
floors in the cloth houses surrounding L'Opera, unwrapping the
treasures, silks and velvets protected by powdering tobacco coloured
tissue, a magpie gathering braid and ribbons that spilled from
split boxes.

　My fingers itched to shape the polished straws that shone like
patent leather to curve and drape velvets, the folds catching light,
enhancing their lustre, still a feast of colour and texture,
unblemished and untouched for over forty years. A hatters' heaven.

PHOTO: DANILO GIULIANI

THE GIFT

The satin ribbons yielded to her touch
    sliding in ripples from the pink laminated box,
    gleaming in the candlelight.
Taking a sip from her champagne,
    she peeled back a haze of white tissue
    layer upon layer.

Nestling in its folds was the tiny exquisite hat.
He had chosen scarlet, his favourite colour.
The feathers trembled as she lifted it –
    to be worn with scarlet stilettos?
Slowly she raised her eyes to his and asked –
"Does it come in beige?".

CHRISTMAS PARTY

The work bench was cleared of hats. Mr Pilkington-Bryer, the Director, checked its surface for pin wastage. Those that had escaped, he prised from the cracks with a determined thumbnail, smiling encouragingly at the grouped workforce, a confirmation that his example should be followed in future.

Four sheets of grade two hat tissue he then smoothed fastidiously on the surface. The group continued to watch.

Oozing benevolence, he placed the sandwich laden paper plates onto the pristine surface (having allocated one and half sandwiches and two mince pies per member of staff).

Next he engaged the post-boy in a ritualistic conversation regarding his mother (who had actually died two years earlier) and football about which he was equally ill-informed.

Mr Pilkington-Bryer terminated the conversation and, glad for the opportunity to escape, the boy rejoined the group, doing so his elbow (unavoidably it appeared) nudged the cherished box of pins scattering them to the floor.

GOING SOLO

With one week's rent and a can of gold spray paint I opened a shop. The shop was a realisation of my fantasy and the fantasy necessitated rather a lot of gilding. The walls just had to be gold and ivory Regency stripe. Then, of course, gold mirrors were a must as were the chandeliers and hat stands.

The curtains and drapes dividing the workroom and showroom were ivory satin. A spotlight in the window displayed a single Sylvia Fletcher creation with the first Sylvia Fletcher label sewn firmly in place. The window sparkled like a diamond between the Busy Bee shoe repairer and the hardware store lighting up pots and pans stacked outside providing a moment of frivolity to women who stood with carrier bags of groceries at their feet.

All this splendour was contained in a space the size of an average bathroom. To be absolutely honest it was half a shop with a hardboard partition wall which had a two foot gap at the top enabling Eric, who rented the other half, to fire paper clips and miscellaneous objects including, on one occasion, a half eaten cheese sandwich, over the top.

I persuaded him that the missile joke, of which he never appeared to tire, would not be appreciated, (in fact there would be a serious threat to his manhood), if he were to take aim when I had a client. Or, if he gave just one of his constant renditions of 'Where Did You Get That Hat?' which he also found side-splittingly funny.

From this Aladdin's Cave I developed a successful business supplying boutiques, Liberty and Harvey Nichols … in spite of Eric.

Ocelot trilby by Sylvia Fletcher, c.1968

COLLEGE

"Hats don't suit me!" she said, facing the mirror in the showroom. With her feet together, clenched fists and an expression that would not sit well under any hat, Mrs Lamberhurst has thrown down the gauntlet. I prepare for the charge, and positioning my scarlet cape at arms length, I step sideways, parrying, until she tires of the game, her jaw relaxes and the furrows clear. Then I produce my ultimate weapon . . .

The perfect hat.

PHOTO: JULIAN MARSHALL

COBWEBS

Across a scarlet mouth,
a wisp of veil,
woven a century past with guile,
casts an eternal spell.

GARDEN PARTY

The lawn was bedded
    with bunched guests.
Hats flowering.
Their colourful brims
    shading provocative eyes
    as from frilled bed linen.

PHOTO: DANILO GIULIANI

PHOTO: DANILO GIULIANI

ROSE

A rose, stamens dipped in crystal dust,
showers silk petals
onto enveloping folds of champagne satin
glossy as caramel,
secured with a breath of thread and placed just so.

DEERSTALKER AT DUSK

A flutter of hooves and you move
towards the enveloping corners of the night.
Stay.

ASCOT

Ascot gallops towards me nostrils flared.
The race begins.
Armed only with a thimble and tape measure
I grasp the reins.
In a flurry of colours and silks I negotiate the course,
   the intricacies of tulle or veiling,
   satin or straw, a flower or feathers or both.
The last order is nested in tissue.
It's neck and neck. A photo finish.
In a fizz of champagne bubbles
   and the waft of air kissing,
   the well toned rumps
   disappear in the distance and Ascot passes.
For the fiftieth year I raise my glass
   and make my fiftieth vow 'never again'.

FASHION DRAWING: BRUCE OLDFIELD, 2009

Ascot

Ascot

PHOTOS: JULIAN MARSHALL

INSPIRATION

On the backs of tired envelopes,
cheque books, taxi receipts
and final demands,
are sown the seeds
of my fantasies.

SUNDAY

The day's a gift.
The ribbons, loosely tied,
would unravel at a touch.
My fingers are reluctant.

My pen waits.

UNIMPORTANT MATTER

The linen basket has thrown up
in the bathroom.
Clean washing, all elbows and knees,
waits to be folded.
Bags of shopping on the kitchen floor
spread their weight
and settle down for the night
. . . I write . . . .

To swim thirty two lengths twice a week at the local pool head to toe with other swimmers could be a mind-numbing exercise, but not for me.

I am not easily distracted by the rubber caps and goggles of the other swimmers, their heads, as they bob past, can be adorned (before submerging again) in a variety of possibilities for my next collection.

Fascinators, straws and felts surface undamaged by a ducking, to have an extra feather or loop added (or in some cases removed, as I have never been known to over garnish).

As you might have guessed I have never progressed beyond the slow lane.

The women circle the table nestling their various shaped arses into cushioned chairs like contented hens on eggs. Wine bubbles from the neck of a bottle as they shuffle pads, papers, files – the month's offering of their work. A waft of thick crusted bread and a variety of cheeses promises a good lunch, but the real feast is the three hours when they can indulge in poems, prose, stories and autobiographies, luxuriate in fantasy, gorge like pigs on one sentence, one word – a rose scented bath snatched from a busy day, with a little guilt. No-one's mother, daughter or wife. Free to take the biggest piece of cake, disclose an addiction, admit a lover. Three hours of excess – forbidden fruit.

LEAVES

His yellow council jacket swayed with the movement
of his broom and the rhythmic swish of the leaves.
"I sweep leaves all day" he said.
"And when I turn round, they're back."
"I sweep leaves all day and dream leaves at night."
"What do you do?"
"Make hats," I said.
"Make hats all day and dream hats at night."
"Where do you get your inspiration from?" he asked.
"Here and there," I said.

PHOTO: DANILO GIULIANI/TRIGGER

DRAGONFLY WINGS

In dreams I bury my face in the scent of you
In dreams you bring the ocean to my lips
Awake you are a thousand dragon fly wings
A crystal reflecting my dreams

SHADOWS

Patterns of lace on bare shoulders
Sunshine through leaves
Beneath a dipping brim
A shawl of shadows

PHOTO DANILO GIULIANI

KISS

I have the memory of a kiss
    light as a butterfly against my face.
In the dark before I sleep it flutters
    leaving wing dust.

PHOTO: SYLVIE TA TA

BISHOP BURTON COLLEGE

STARGAZER

A shaft of winter moonlight blue and silver
   held in its beam specks of shimmering dust,
   the iridescent lustre of an opal in a milk mist.
I stretch out my hands open palmed
   to be kissed by its light and dip into opalescence.
Watching in wonder the colours shimmer
   and play on my fingers,
I lift them to my lips, the essence is sweet
   on my tongue and stirs an unslaked desire in repose.

PARROT FASHION

"This is my friend Mabeline, she always advises me on my wardrobe. Don't know what I would do without her".

Mabeline was wearing a full length felt cloak that she had either bought at the local craft fair or embroidered herself whilst waiting for the last batch of currant preserve to set. She swung it confidently across her ample bosom taking with it two hat stands and her friend's handbag.

"Might I say", said Mabeline, *"that we have tried on every hat in London and there would have been some disastrous choices had I not been there".* She gave a hearty wink to her friend who was looking rather tired.

"You are obviously an asset", I agreed.

"Might I say", said Mabeline, *"that I have noticed you featured veils in your new Spring collection".*

"Vintage silk veiling", I enthused, *"romantic, flirtatious".*

"Irritating", said Mabeline, *"now I have in mind something more 'bowsey wowsey' with a rose".*

"It may not sit well with the pinstripe suit", I said.

"But might I say Sylvia, that it will have a softening effect, eclectic".

"I admit that indeed it would be that and was tempted to suggest that something like a parrot could then work very well, add that splash of colour, even offer a third opinion".

A parrot apparition manifested itself on the brim of the 'bowsey wowsey' that Mabeline was placing (at completely the wrong angle) on her victim's head.

"Might I say", said Mabeline, *"très chic".*

"Très chic", said the parrot preening its feathers.

"Who's a pretty girl then", I squawked, getting into the moment. My clients edged towards the door as the parrot and I swayed from one foot to the other. I had deflected a Mabeline.

WEDDING SONG

I want vanilla satin
    with lace beneath unseen,
A necklace with a diamond clasp
    and knickers trimmed in green.
A bodice fastened with fifty pearls,
    with the sheen of clotted cream
And a man who's good with buttons,
    not just a virgin's dream.

FASCINATOR

A beautiful man in an expensive suit was browsing the showroom
gently picking up the most flamboyant shape in my collection
supporting it on one hand and pivoting it with the other as if it were
on the head of a woman.
He said he was looking for a hat as a gift and I asked the age and
proportions of its wearer.
"She is about your age and size, blonde and pretty like you."
I blushed a little and offered to model some hats for him. Slowly
he studied each creation as I twirled for him placing his hand on
my arm to check the profile. His face often close to mine as he
sometimes gave the hat a little extra tilt or studied the patterns of
the straw. I preened with a black feather fascinator in my hair; we
were two birds of paradise performing a pre-nuptial dance.
He smiled delightedly but chose a fine straw with a large red rose.
"More suitable for the occasion," he said and it was to be gift
wrapped with a large red bow to complement the accompanying
bouquet of twelve red roses and, *"Oh, would it be at all possible
to embroider on the hat ribbon – Will You Marry Me?"*

The wind had penetrated my clothes.

My umbrella, a spine broken flapped like a wounded bat.

From under my trilby escaping strands of hair dripped with rain

A taxi emptied the contents of a small pond onto my legs.

I leaned into the onslaught, eyes streaming, nose streaming.

At the bus stop, through the rain was a figure I recognised.

"Hallo sweetheart" he said, *"You look fabulous in that hat".*

NO! NO! NO! NO!

NO! NO! NO! NO!

No, Mrs Ellismore!

A feather will not add a little something to the design

    and no, the hem of your dress would not make a very nice bow trim.

I'm aware that it's the one you wore when your husband proposed,

    but he's probably forgotten by now, even if he noticed in the first place.

No to a rose and no to your deceased Mother's brooch.

No plumes and no drapes and ostrich is definitely not the answer.

    (I have an allergy to that particular feather).

And it's no to that hat pin.

No, Mrs Ellismore!

NO! NO! NO! NO! NO!

BUMBLE

At two fifteen Bumble entered the showroom.

On the loop end of his lead was Mrs Bunny Brampton-Wick,
   puffing, having climbed four flights of stairs

At a speed she would not necessarily have chosen.

"We are sorry we're late", said Mrs Brampton-Wick ,

"You had your mind set on one of those St James' Park ducks, didn't you old chap".

"Glass of water?" "Yes, I'd love one dear".

"There you are Bumble".

"He has no trouble drinking from a glass you see".

"Such a character".

At this point I must mention that I don't like dogs.

I particularly Don't like dogs in hat shops.

"He's taken to you", said Bunny.

"He doesn't take to everyone".

"Grr", said Bumble.

"Up", said Bunny.

"Up on Mummy's lap old chap".

"He'll need to have his head measured".

Such a character.

SINGLE ROOM

I picked an orange from a tree
   beside my balcony.
I felt its fullness, its heavy flesh.
Enjoyed its sun-ripened colour,
   heightened by dark leaves.
I cradled the fruit in cupped hands,
   breathing in a fragrance
    I longed to share.

I was disconcerted by Miss Maplethorpe. She strongly resembled the much loved comedienne Dawn French; her mannerisms and body language were Dawn French to perfection – a look-alike. I adjusted to this and followed her enthusiastic progress. She pounced on a small black and white hat inappropriate for her and many sizes too small. It teetered ludicrously on her head as she twirled for my approval wide eyed and with a grin of delight. I had hoped that she was joking, but Miss Maplethorpe was serious.

I heard a loud laugh and realised with alarm that it had come from me. It burst like a bubble, a small explosion. It was unprofessional, unprecedented and unforgivable. I attempted to disguise it with a bout of coughing steering her away from the object of her desire to find that her second and third choices were equally unflattering. My client was oblivious to her considerable talent for mimicry as she waved aside any advice that I offered and pirouetted in the second, then third unsuitable hat.

It was too much for me; the effort I made to regain my composure resulted in a tight little scream. Clutching my throat and muttering something about water I escaped to the adjoining workroom where I slid down the wall convulsed with laughter. My assistant took over from me at this point, as I was unable to speak. Later she returned to convey wishes for my recovery from Miss Maplethorpe who recommended a herbal cough mixture and had purchased a small black and white hat.

MOTHER OF THE BRIDE

There is a 'Mother of the Bride' orbiting the showroom.

She is buzzing from hat to hat, not savouring each creation like a humming bird or a bee, but with wasp-like agitation.

I attempt to catch the elusive creature.

My pursuit is hampered by scatterings of designer carrier bags which have formed an expensive obstacle course.

My attempts to calm her have failed.

The glass of iced water with lemon, thinly sliced, remains untouched on the table.

My client is out of control.

It is now necessary for me to take the initiative.

I throw the window open wide giving her the opportunity to fly off into St James Street before she damages herself on the furniture.

MOLLY

A fuschia blooms in Molly's garden, filtering sunshine,
    patterning the window in her kitchen where the pan lids click.
On the sill a broken twig, heavy with buds,
    has been rescued and survives in a glass.
It throws a shadow across a faded photograph of Molly and Albert
    dancing at the company's annual 'do'.
The black chiffon dress, soft as bloom on a blueberry,
    clings to her legs.

I chose pink for Molly, not lavender, grey or beige.
Molly is splendid in fuschia and has blossomed in my feisty pink hat.

MY WIFE DOESN'T SUIT GREEN

"Now this is what she will be wearing."
"It's our son's wedding and we're looking
for something classic with a sensible brim."
"It's a style that has always flattered her."
"Nothing green, my wife doesn't suit green!"
"It will be accessorised with a brown
crocodile handbag that was my mother's."
I have persuaded her that it is entirely suitable."
"Now if you would first measure her head
she would like to visit the Ladies Room."

MRS LATIMER-SNIPE'S RENOVATION

Mrs Latimer-Snipe here. I bought a hat from you eleven years ago, you won't remember me.

I do actually.

I was a little indecisive on that occasion. I believe I tried on every hat in the shop. It took at least four visits or was it five?

Five, Mrs Latimer-Snipe, definitely five.

I really believe you were as delighted as me when I found the perfect hat in the sale bucket reduced to five pounds. I'm phoning because my boxer Wilson has chewed through the ribbon and it needs to be replaced.

If you would like to leave it at the front desk we will certainly do that for you.

I prefer to make an appointment with you, I feel it needs the designer's input, you gave birth to it so to speak - your baby.

I did indeed but as it has almost reached puberty I feel there is little need for my specific nurturing, so to speak.

I have been debating whether to have a knot or a bow on the replacement ribbon and have often wondered if it should not be half a centimetre narrower and we could revisit the colour.

Perhaps the flavour would be more relevant in the circumstances, might I suggest that you bring Wilson in and you decide together.

I would like one of your beautiful laminated boxes to store it in and you may need to post it to me if I am not able to collect. I assume this is part of your excellent aftercare service and therefore no charge will be involved. I am in London on 27th August and would like to make an appointment with you for that day.

I am so sorry but I won't be here at that time, I am about to take early retirement.

Oh! When did you decide that?

At approximately the time you said that you could not decide between a knot or a bow on your ribbon Mrs Latimer-Snipe!

I BALANCED THE HAT ON MY HEAD

I balanced the hat on my head.
Studied it.
Held it against my skin.
I had chosen the colour of warmed pearls
    edged with a pattern of shells.
It was small and tilted to allow a kiss,
    throwing just enough shadow to hide my eyes.

PHOTOS: DANILO GIULIANI

HOTEL 'LE COQ BLEU' FRANCE

Emptying the summerhouse in the Spring was a mistake. It has since become occupied by a woman in a large brimmed hat.

We first noticed the net curtains and a rotary clothes line. She came with 'Saga' for a cheap weekend break although I assumed she had been counted back on the coach with the others. I should have been suspicious when during her stay she placed a milk order, one pint every other day semi-skimmed to be left at the end of the garden.

She will not go home. We have tried smoking her out but it caused only an irritating cough. We asked our Mayor to persuade her to leave but he said she was making his wife a sexy little pillbox with a veil and a bunch of cherries over one eye and that he was rather looking forward to that.

He did write to her family, but they replied saying, by now she had made each of them a hat for every possible occasion and that as a family, they were severely over-hatted. So they would be grateful if we would hang on to her, provide her with a regular supply of feathers and glue to enable her to make stylish headwear for guests and provide stimulating conversation during the three day wait for the Boeuf Bourguignon.

We did try this last Thursday with more enthusiasm on her part than the guests, and it seems we have now committed ourselves to an Easter Bonnet competition. Information for this event can be obtained from the large poster hanging in the hotel foyer where we previously enjoyed a Matisse, (along with her business cards and brochures).

For this event she has made me a rather jaunty wide-brimmed panama in a soft buttermilk colour, made of the finest straw and sweeping slightly to one side. The band is a James Lock stripe and she advised that I wear it slightly.....

RED

Red never whispers. It's first in a queue.
Sits alone in a restaurant with ease.
At a party red is the last to arrive
And never the first to leave.

Red is carnival, Christmas, flamenco,
Rides a horse on the carousel.
Red is fireworks and showtime
Takes the finale in a fabulous hat.

YELLOW

I found a yellow marble.
Tiny bubbles of memory suspended in glass.
A golden eye, bright with glorious days.

WHITE

Mute as snow
and fleeting as frost.
It has the trickery
of a bridal veil
and will slip away
like a child's fairy tale.

MILLINER'S WISH

When I am very old
I shall adjust people's hats
in the street
if I can reach

BY APPOINTMENT TO H.R.H. THE DUKE OF EDINBURGH
HATTERS

BY APPOINTMENT TO H.R.H. THE PRINCE OF WALES
HATTERS

BRIAN TOWERS

Special thanks to Royal hatters James Lock & Co. on whose prestigious rafters I have perched for 15 years,
for their enthusiasm and support in making its facilities available to promote this book.

Acknowledgements
Peter Cope, design & art direction.
Bruce Oldfield, for providing fashion drawing 'Ascot 2009'.
Brian Towers, for providing his watercolour painting of James Lock & Co. shopfront.
Little, Brown & Co, publishers, for permitting the use of their copyrighted illustrations.
Hans Feurer & Vogue/Condé Nast Publications Ltd for permitting the use of 'Deerstalker at Dusk' image.
Photographers Danilo Giuliani, Julian Marshall, Ed Reeve and Sylvie Ta Ta.
Edge Design and Trigger for releasing photographic images.
Profile Model Management for permitting the appearance of its models
Ganchimeg Bayarsaikhan, Lyzzie Kerry, Mimi Muller, Leanne Nagle, Angèle Sassy and Sylvia Valcikova.
MOT Models for permitting the appearance of its model Chrystal Rudd.
Union Models for permitting the appearance of its model Jasmine Hemsle.